P9-BZU-073

Herbal Crafts

Silverleaf Press Books are available exclusively
through Independent Publishers Group.

For details write or telephone
Independent Publishers Group, 814 North Franklin St.
Chicago, IL 60610, (312) 337-0747
Silverleaf Press
8160 South Highland Drive
Sandy, Utah 84093

ISBN: 978-1-933317-45-8

Herbal Crafts

More than 60 Simple Projects to Beautify Your Home and Body

Jessie Hawkins

Table of Contents

INTRODUCTION

Herbs have always been intriguing to me. I was first introduced to them at age 13 while volunteering at a history museum. Our summer project included tending an old-fashioned herb garden and making lavender wands as accessories for Early American costumes.

Now, as a Master Herbalist, I have to say that the amazement is still there. These tiny plants pack such a punch, yield the most beautiful flowers, and hold such a long tradition in cultures worldwide. Not only do they have natural properties that still baffle the modern scientific mind, but no dish is complete without a few herbs added in the mix. Herbs dry out beautifully, making them ideal for crafting and decorating. And there is nothing quite like the pleasure of growing these little beauties yourself.

In this book, I have included my favorite herbal crafts for herbs of all seasons. Many of these crafts are so simple that my children can assist me with them. Others are more complex and require my full attention. All of them, however, make great additions to our home. And friends and family always love the gifts we have made for them.

The crafts included can be made with easy-to-find materials, available at your local hobby store or health food store. Herbs can be grown in your own backyard or purchased either online or locally.

Above all, have a great time crafting with these special plants. And remember to take the time to be in awe of these wondrous creations.

Jessie Hawkins, Master Herbalist

FRAGRANCE

herbal scents create the perfect mood

Pomanders

Pomanders are an important part of traditional holiday decor. The word pomander dates back to the middle ages, but they were used centuries before.

You will need:

3 oranges (can also use other citrus fruits)
1/2 cup whole cloves
1/2-inch (13mm) wide satin ribbon
optional: small bay leaves

Method:

1. Cover the oranges with cloves, leaving a narrow space all around the circumference so that ribbon can be tied around it once it is dried. Stud the oranges with cloves, leaving a small space between each one to allow for shrinkage. You may have to pierce the skin with a darning needle to get the dried cloves firmly embedded.
2. If desired, tuck the bay leaves between the cloves.
3. Put the oranges in a paper bag and leave them in a dark, dry place where air is circulating for three weeks to a month. By then it should be thoroughly dry.
4. Tie the ribbon around the orange to hang the pomander.

Potpourri

It comes as a surprise to find that "potpourri," a word so evocative of gentle fragrance, actually means "rotted pot." The word is derived from the French verb "pourir" which means "to grow rotten." The name came about by reason of the method once used to retain the fragrance of flowers and herbs.

Collecting and Drying Flower and Leaves

No matter how sweetly scented they may be, do not be seduced by white flowers—they can look very dingy when dried.

You can dry violets, roses, lavender, rosemary, marigolds, port-wine magnolia flowers, carnations, mints, marjoram, balm, verbena, chamomile, costmary, woodruff, bergamot, nasturtiums, and scented leaved geraniums. And, for their blue color, cornflowers, forget-me-nots, and plumbago flowers work well. Much of the pleasure of making potpourri is the quiet time spent in the garden making choices.

When you have decided which ones you want to dry, collect a number of large, screw-topped jars—one for each type of flower, plus an extra one, and keep them on one side.

Drying

1. Choose somewhere quiet and dry—a seldom-used bedroom, the back of a garden shed. You will need a large piece of muslin and an old chair. Cut the muslin to the size made by the four upturned legs. Tie each corner of the muslin to a leg. This will make a tray on which the herbs can be laid. Air will be able to flow above and beneath the fabric.

2. In the mornings when the sun has dried the dew but has not yet become hot, pick your flowers and leaves and spread them out on the muslin, each different variety in its own spot. Leave them to become dry and lightly crisp, then store each one in a labeled, screw-topped jar.

Continue doing this until you feel you have enough material.

Discard anything that has become brown—the leaves should have retained their green, the flowers, their color.

Quick and Easy Potpourri

Potpourri is a tool every sixteenth-century housewife used to refresh the home, adding a touch of her own gardening skills. Many of these herbs are grown in gardens today and can charm the inside long after their outdoor growing season is over.

You will need:

2 cups dried rose petals
2 cups dried lavender flowers
2 tablespoons dried lemon verbena leaves
2 tablespoons dried rosemary
2 tablespoons orris root powder
½ teaspoon powdered gum benzoin
2 drops lavender oil

1. Mix together all the ingredients but the last one. When nicely blended, add the oil a drop at a time, stirring continuously, to spread it through the mix evenly.

2. Tip the materials into a large jar, filling it only loosely and store in a dark, warm, dry place. Ideally you should visit it every day for the next five weeks to give it a good shake. This is important—impatience doesn't pay off.

3. The final potting should be in the prettiest and most imaginative container you can find. There are perforated ones made for the purpose, but I find that to get the best from any potpourri it is best to take off the lid and shake the contents around at strategic moments. The perfume needs to be released to drift on the air. The fragrance is subtler than that of incense sticks, which make it seem as though you are trying too hard.

Herbal Potpourri

This scent makes a great addition to a kitchen or garden room. The citrus and herbal blend is strong, yet mellow.

You will need:

2 cups lemon verbena
1 cup lemon balm
1/4 cup orange peel
1/3 cup lavender
1/2 cup sage
1/2 cup whole bay leaves
1/3 cup rosemary
1/3 cup thyme
1/3 cup calendula flowers
1/3 cup chamomile flowers
2 cinnamon sticks, crushed
5 drops each of lavender, lemon, and sweet orange essential oil
4 drops lemon verbena essential oil

1. In a large bowl, mix everything together.
2. Place in a sealed container or bag and leave sealed for 2 weeks for the scents to blend.
3. Pour into a flowerpot or vase.

Lavender Rose Potpourri

Roses and lavender flowers have always been popular as the base of a potpourri because they can keep their perfume for a long time without the aid of a fixative, but today though the scent of the lavender is as strong as it ever was, how often do we find gardens drenched with the scent of great, pink cabbage roses as they were in earlier times? To get a real rose scent today you have to search—the ones with the strongest perfume seem to be the single, dark red roses. If all else fails, use essential oils.

You will need:

2 cups rose petals
1 cup lavender buds
¼ cup rosemary
¼ cup thyme
½ cup whole bay leaves
¼ cup marjoram
4 cinnamon sticks, crushed
¼ cup juniper berries
2 tablespoons orange peel
3 drops each of geranium essential oil, lavender essential oil, and sweet orange essential oil

1. In a large bowl, mix everything together.
2. Place in a sealed container or bag and leave sealed for 2 weeks for the scents to blend.
3. Pour into a shallow bowl or vase. This blend makes plenty to fill several rooms with a coordinating scent.

Cinnamon Candles

These cinnamon candles add a rustic touch to the holiday season, making them the perfect gift for the nature-loving person in your life. The cinnamon fragrance is subtle, but can be heightened by using a cinnamon-scented candle as your base.

You will need:

3-inch (8cm) wide pillar candle (about 5 inches tall)
12–14 cinnamon sticks
1 votive candle (white)
paintbrush

1. Begin by arranging the cinnamon sticks around the pillar candle evenly.
2. Once you have chosen their location, set them next to that spot on the candle.
3. Melt the votive candle in a warm oven.
4. Working quickly, paint the hot wax from the votive candle onto the sides of the cinnamon and the pillar candle. Press the cinnamon sticks onto the candle, while the wax is still hot. As the wax cools, it will serve as your glue, holding the sticks in place.
5. Finish by painting the remaining melted wax over the cinnamon sticks, making sure to leave an even finish and to cover any loose spots in the candle.

Note: The candle can also be melted in a microwave, but be sure to check on it often.

Scented Candles

The fragrance of a scented candle is light—much more subtle than that of an incense stick—the soft glow and the drifting perfume make magic on a quiet evening.

You will need:

Leftover pieces of candle or some inexpensive white ones
Some thin string or wicking
Some skewers or chopsticks
Some muslin sachets of your favorite scented herb, to which you have attached a length of strong cotton. This helps you remove the sachets from the hot wax.

1. Place the sachets in an old saucepan with the cotton trailing over the edge and assemble your molds. This is where ingenuity comes in. Each mold must have a hole in the center of its base for the wick to be fitted. You will be very lucky if you find anything which will give you a tall, straight or tapering candle but there are many different sizes of waxed food cartons which will do.

2. Coast the inside of each mold with vegetable oil so that the finished candle will slip out easily.

3. Melt your candles in the top of a double saucepan or a jug in the microwave oven. When melted but not too hot, carefully remove any bits of wick.

4. Reheat the wax.

5. While it is heating, tie a piece of string or wick to as many skewers of chopsticks as you have molds, centering the string on the skewer.

6. Feed the string through the hole on the bottom of the molds as you lay the skewers or chopsticks across the top of the mold. Pull the string down so that it hangs, taut and vertical.

7. When the wax is hot but not boiling, pour it into the saucepan containing the sachets. The heat must be high enough to extract the herb juices that carry the fragrance.

8. Let the wax cool slightly and sniff it. If you don't think the fragrance is strong enough, add a very few drops of the appropriate essential oil. Remove the muslin sachets by the strong cotton.

9. Pour the wax into the molds making sure that the wick stays in the center. Leave until cold and hard. Cut the wick and remove the skewer. Remove the candle from the mold. The advantage of using cartons is that they can be peeled away if the candle is stubborn about leaving the mold.

Lover's Incense

Fragrant smoke has risen to the heavens as long as man has prayed to his gods—sweet herbs were burned as offering to Ra, the Egyptian sun-god. The North American Indians not only used smoke to send signals to each other but burned sweet herbs to purify themselves and their environment as they sent up prayers to the Great Spirit. Today we burn incense in our homes, not so much with religion in mind as the pleasure given and the atmosphere created by the fragrant smoke. The scent is clean—the air seems purer.

You will need:

½ cup powdered lavender flowers
½ cup powdered rosemary flowers
¼ cup powdered rose petals
½ cup sandalwood bark powder
½ cup water
1 teaspoon potassium nitrate
tragacanth powder to mix

1. Mix the dried herbs with the bark powder.
2. Mix the potassium nitrate with a little water. Add tragacanth powder and mix to a smooth paste, adding more water if needed.
3. Add the dried herbs and continue mixing adding water and tragacanth powder as needed until you have a smooth paste which can be formed into firm shapes.

Fragrance Logs

Fragrance logs make a perfect housewarming gift. They also can be used as party favors for a holiday gathering. These little touches add a lot to the traditional warm winter fire.

You will need:
raffia ribbon
8 stalks dried lavender
8 stalks dried rosemary
8 stalks dried sage

1. Arrange each group of herbs together, alternating stems.
2. Begin looping the raffia around the bunches until they are tightly tied together.
3. Finish with a secure knot, so the "log" does not come apart while burning.

Have a fun time experimenting with different herbs for this gift. If you grow your own, choose your favorite aromatic herbs from the garden to dry out and bundle for your friends.

Drawer Liners

Drawer liners serve many purposes. They decorate an otherwise drab environment and contain light scents that add a unique fragrance to your clothing or bed linens.

You will need:

enough 12 x 12-inch (30x30cm) squares of scrapbooking paper to line the drawers in your bureau

½ ounce (14g) bottle essential oil (lavender, geranium or sweet orange work best)

1. Line drawers with paper, cutting edges to fit exactly.
2. Drop essential oils into corners and center, one drop at a time. Aim for 3–4 drops per drawer. Remember, essential oils are very potent.
3. Refreshed the scent every 6–9 months.

Closet Sachets

Tie this sachet onto a hanger in your closet or tuck it into a drawer to freshen up the scent of your clothing or closet space.

You will need:
muslin drawstring bag
¼ cup dried fragrant herbs

Simply toss the herbs together into the muslin bag and tie to a coat hanger or hook in the closet.

Try using different herbs for different effects.
Lavender: calming, relaxing
Mint: natural rodent repellant
Chamomile: apple-like scent
Lemon balm: herbal citrus scent
Orange peel: fresh, clean scent

Did you know...? **Essential oils are not really oils at all—at least, not as we know them. Also known as "volatile oils," essential oils are the distillates or extracts from herbs and other plants. True essential oils can be costly, but there is no substitute for the original oil. Fragrance oils do not offer the aromatherapy benefits that true oils offer.**

Dryer Sheets

With so many scents to choose from, essential oils are an ideal choice for making your own dryer sheets. These are reusable and won't damage your dryer over time, like some commercial sheets can. You also have the flexibility of making them as strong or light as you prefer and of changing scents to suit your mood.

You will need:
old washcloths
essential oils of choice (I like lavender, sweet orange, clary sage, or geranium.)

1. Drop 2–3 drops of essential oil onto washcloth.
2. Toss into dryer with wet clothes and dry as usual.
3. If you plan on changing the scent, wash washcloth in warm water before adding the new scents.

Room Spray

Air fresheners are much more natural when they are made with scents that are already common to your home. Try blending scents to match the herbs in season in your kitchen or outdoor garden.

You will need:
2–4 ounces (57–113g) glass spray bottle
distilled water
one of the following blends:

Herbal Essential Oil Blend

¾ teaspoon lavender essential oil
½ teaspoon basil essential oil
½ teaspoon lemon verbena essential oil

Floral Essential Oil Blend

3/4 teaspoon geranium essential oil
1 teaspoon sweet orange essential oil
1/4 teaspoon clary sage essential oil

1. Fill the bottle with the distilled water, leaving an inch from the top.
2. Add one of the oil blends and shake well to blend.
3. Remember to shake well before using to disperse the oils.

Linen Powder

Drift off to sweet dreams with this linen refresher. I love using this powder between washings to freshen up my linens. Blankets and towels still smell delightful when pulled out several weeks after they've been washed.

You will need:
½ cup cornstarch
½ cup arrowroot powder
¼ cup each dried lavender and chamomile
5 drops sweet orange essential oil
decorative jar

1. In a food processor, grind the herbs into a fine powder. Scrape down the sides and process until there are no large pieces left.
2. Add the cornstarch and essential oil and process until well blended.
3. Scoop into the jar.

To use: Sprinkle 1/4 teaspoon of powder onto sheets or a blanket and shake to disperse.

Lavender Cones

An arrangement of lavender makes a pretty, scented decorative feature.

You will need:

A large, well-opened pine-cone
Short stalks of lavender flowers
A small cork
Varnish
Glue

1. Varnish the cone, and when dry glue it to the cork to make a base.
2. Dip the ends of the lavender stalks into the glue and push into the spaces of the opened cones. Pack the stalks in tightly and evenly.
3. When you are satisfied with the shape, add a few drops of essential oil of lavender to increase the fragrance.

Instead of using the cork base, you could attach ribbon to the cone and hang it by a loop in a warm room for the fragrance to be released and circulate.

DECORATING

wreaths, garlands, topiaries, and more beautiful herbal designs

Lavender Stalks

Not only are these stalks a great visual addition to the mantle, but the classic lavender scent can freshen up any room.

You will need:

30–35 dried lavender stalks
florist ribbon
½ yard (.5m) of 1-inch (2.5cm) satin ribbon
large knife or florist scissors

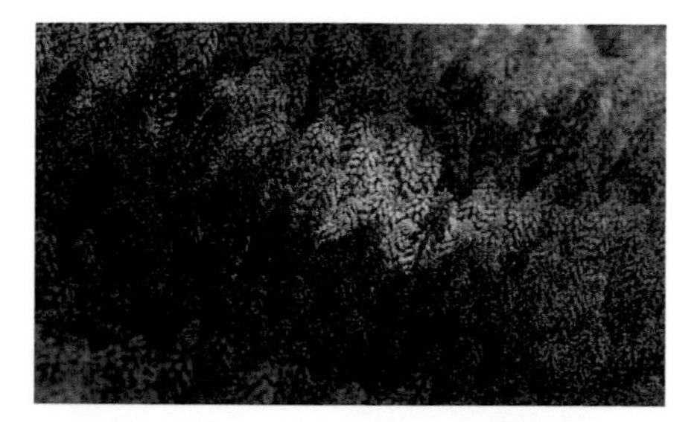

1. Arrange the stalks as a bouquet with the tallest flowers in the center gently drifting downward.
2. Tie together with the florist wire.
3. Cut the stems exactly flat across the bottom.
4. Holding the flowers in one hand, and the stems in the other, gently twist 1/4 turn, so the stems curve around the base.
5. Trim the bottom again to be sure it is still flat.
6. Cover the wire with the satin ribbon and a large bow.

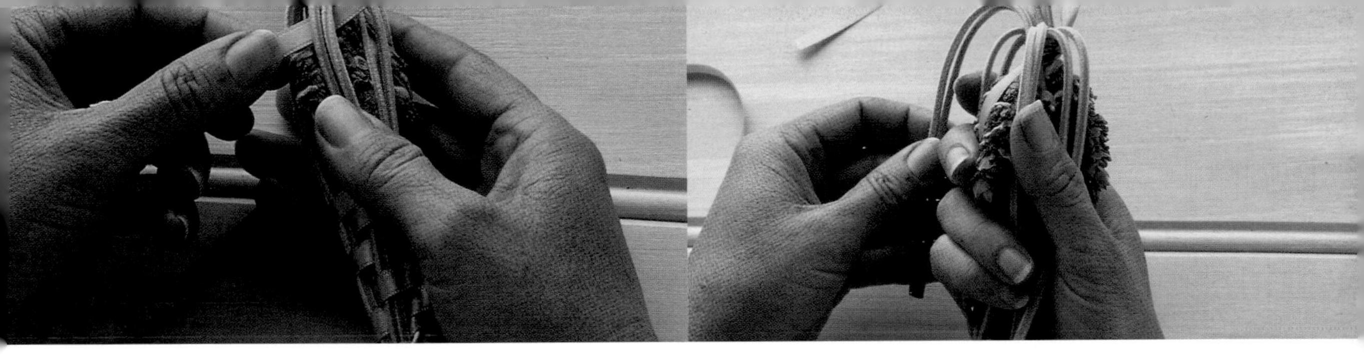

Lavender Wands

Lavender wands were used before the age of deodorants. A lady would tuck a wand into her dress or basket to enhance her odor. Lavender is also an effective moth repellent that will keep your closet or drawer moth-free and smelling fresh.

You will need:

20 young, fresh, long-stalked spikes of lavender flowers (Don't use old ones, they are not pliable enough.)

39 inches (1m) of narrow lavender-colored ribbon

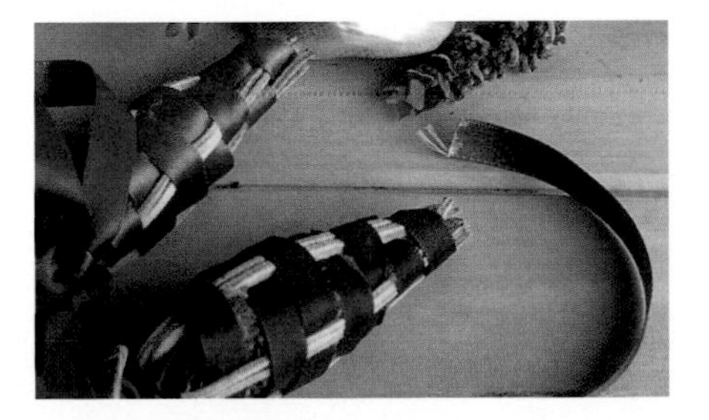

1. Arrange the lavender stalks in equal lengths.
2. Tie the ribbon tightly just below the flower spikes with one end of the ribbon short and the other long. The short end should be about 8 inches (20cm).
3. Take the long end of the ribbon upwards to extend beyond the top of the flower spikes.
4. Bend 10 spikes, in groups of two upwards, from just below the knotted ribbon and arrange them to enclose the flower heads completely. Trim off any surplus.
5. Starting at the top and working down, weave the long end of the ribbon through them horizontally. Pull it tight—the flowers will shrink as they dry. Cover them completely.
6. Tie the two ends of ribbon into a bow.

a wreath **like this looks very pretty when fresh and, if kept out of too much light and in a well-ventilated spot, will keep its looks as it dries.**

Fresh Herbal Wreath

Festive wreaths celebrating birthdays, wedding anniversaries, weddings, christenings and all joyful occasions are easily made, and if herbs and flowers which dry easily made, and if herbs and flowers which dry easily are used, will give pleasure for quite a long time.

You will need:

A large bunch of preferred herbs, such as sprigs of bay, lavender, sage, thyme, wormwood, rosemary, tarragon, hyssop, marjoram, mint, and the colorful flowers of borage, bergamot, catnip, chamomile, roses, santolina, golden rod, meadowsweet, plumbago, etc.

sphagnum moss

floral wire

wire wreath base

1. Cover a wire wreath base with sphagnum moss so that the wire is completely concealed and fix it in place with fine insulating wire.

2. Cut herb sprigs all the same length and insert them in the wire working from left to right (or right to left, if you work better that way). All sprigs must face the same way. You can use them mixed or in successive groups of different herbs.

3. Bind them in place with wire. Wind wire around the stem of each sprig, cut off and insert in the wreath. Estimate length of stem and wire needed to make the best effect. Cover base.

Bay Laurel Wreath

For many years bay leaves have symbolized victory and triumph. From ancient Greek Olympic crowns to your own present-day doorway, bay laurel offers a feeling of pride and simplicity. This wreath complements any decor and is so easy to make.

You will need:
10–12 very large sprigs of bay laurel, dried
floral wire
1 yard (1m) brown satin ribbon (1-inch/2.5cm wide)

1. Make a base for the wreath with the floral wire. Wrap it into a 10-inch circle, 3 strands thick.
2. With the wire, begin attaching the bay sprigs onto the frame gently overlapping each sprig until the entire frame is covered. The final sprig may need to be tucked into the first one.
3. Loop the ribbon around the top of the frame, and tie a bow onto a hook on the wall 6 inches above the wreath.

Springtime Wreath

Nothing says springtime like a wreath of fresh, springy herbal flowers. Welcome the season with this easy-to-make, beautiful decoration.

You will need:
straw wreath (12-inch/30cm works well)
sprigs of fresh flowering herbs (I like to use whatever is in season in the garden.)
floral wire
ribbon

1. Rinse the herbs.
2. Group herbs into small bunches of like flowers.
3. Begin attaching bunches, one at a time to the straw wreath base using the floral wire. Make sure the stems all face the same direction.
4. Tuck the last bunch of stems into the first, so that the stems cannot be seen and the wreath is completely covered.
5. Finish with the satin ribbon, tying it into a bow on the wreath or as a loop to hang from.

If allowed to hang in indirect sunlight, the herbs will eventually dry out, leaving a keepsake that can be reused again and again. Be sure that the herbs are completely dry before storing.

Garland of Dried Herbs

To make a garland of any size, a large amount of material is needed so it is necessary to think ahead and stockpile ready for the day the garland is to be created.

You will need:

Bunches of tansy, golden rod, rosemary, chamomile, bergamot, mixed with sprigs of thyme and lavender. Small colored glass balls, bells, ribbons and other baubles add to the decoration.

1. Tiny bunches of herbs are tied together with wire and laid horizontally on a plait of raffia, their stems hiding that of the preceding bunch and are wired into place.
2. It is a long and quite difficult process as the wiring is tricky. Each little bunch should be as colorful as possible and the baubles used freely.

Dyed Yarn

Knitters always love to find a new and unique yarn to use for something special. With a little time and creativity, you can hand dye yarns using herbs from your own garden. Give these colorful yarns as gifts with a personal touch. For an even more unique yarn, look at a farmers market or ask nearby farmers for hand spun yarn to dye.

You will need:

yarn, very loosely tied (remember the solution has to reach all parts of the yarn)
stainless steel pot
½ tablespoon cream of tarter
1 pound (.5kg) of fresh herbs
wooden spoon

1. Mix the herbs and 1 gallon water in the pot and bring to a boil.
2. Reduce heat to medium low.
3. Stir in the cream of tarter.
4. Add the yarn and stir with the spoon until well coated.
5. Allow to gently boil 15–20 minutes, stirring every 3–5 minutes.
6. Remove from the water and let dry.
7. When dry, rinse until the water runs clear, then hang to dry again.

Different herbs can achieve different shades or colors. Here is a list of common colors:

Red: dandelion, St. Johns Wort, sweet woodruff, hops, potentilla

Yellow: turmeric, broom, goldenrod, sage, tansy, yarrow

Blue: elder flowers, elecampane, indigo, woad

Brown: burdock, comfrey, fennel, onion, geranium, onion, poplar

Orange: lichen, bloodroot, golden marguerite, sunflower

Green: rosemary, yarrow, rosemary, agrimony, angelica, betony, coltsfoot, foxglove, marjoram, rosemary, tansy, yarrow

Black: black walnut, alder,black walnut, yarrow

Gold: goldenrod, plantain, safflower, agrimony,

Pink: bloodroot, chicory, madder, pokeweed, sorrel

Gray: poplar, raspberry, sunflower (petals), yarrow

Purple: Geranium, lady's bedstraw.

Spring Topiary

Traditionally topiaries are plants trained to fit a wire shape in its pot. With careful training and trimming, beautiful shapes can unfold. This spring topiary is a bit less time-consuming, but every bit as beautiful to see.

You will need:

4-inch (10cm) flowerpot
Styrofoam cone-shaped floral base
a stick (about ½ inch/1cm in diameter)
enough floral foam to fill the pot
hot glue gun
herbal flowers and leaves:
- *calendula*
- *lavender*
- *red and pink roses*
- *bay leaves*
- *moss*

1. Secure the foam into the pot with hot glue.
2. Secure the stick into the center of the foam in the flowerpot.
3. Cover the exposed foam with moss, using the hot glue gun.
4. Attach the cone to the top end of the stick, leaving 3 inches as a "stem."
5. Begin with the largest flowers and attach the herbs to the cone base, using the glue gun.
6. After all flowers are attached, glue the bay leaves among the flowers randomly.
7. If desired, attach a satin ribbon to the flowerpot.

Using darker autumn herbs and leaves, these instructions can be adapted to create an autumn topiary. Try bay leaves, chamomile flowers, mini red or yellow apples, brightly colored fall leaves, and so much more!

Door Vase or Basket

Add a subtle welcome on interior doors with these mini door vases. Not only do they look beautiful, but the subtle fragrance can also freshen up any space.

You will need:
6–8 sprigs fresh or dried herbs
16 inches (41cm) wide satin ribbon (wired)
5-inch (13cm) square of card stock
floral tape
parchment paper (5-inch/13cm square)

1. If using fresh stems, rinse the flowers.
2. Fold two sides of the card stock together to form a cone.
3. Tape together on the inside of the cone.
4. On either side, punch a hole and thread the ribbon through, leaving 2 inches of ribbon hanging out each hole. Tie the two ends together. This will make the handle to hang it from the doorknob.
5. Arrange the stems into a bouquet inside the parchment, then slip the parchment into the card stock cone.

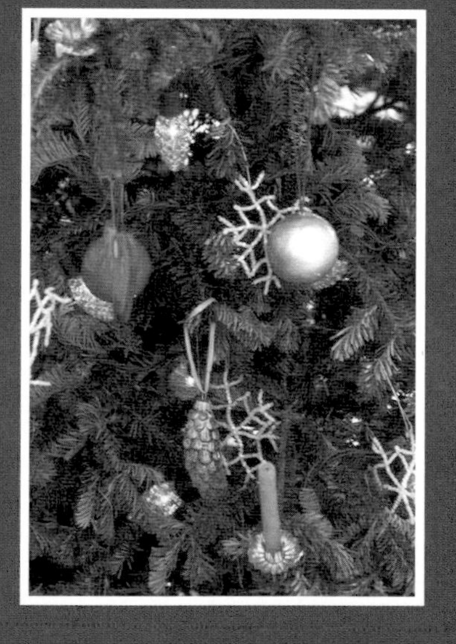

Christmas Ornaments

These natural ornaments look beautiful against a dark green natural tree, and they offer a unique aroma to the holiday trimmings.

You will need:
Styrofoam balls
an assortment of herbs, including lavender, rosemary, chamomile, calendula, dried roses, and bay leaves
hot glue gun
ribbon

1. For each ball, begin by gluing the largest flowers and leaves to the ball first.
2. Add herbs until the ball is completely covered.
3. Loop the ribbon and glue both ends to the top of the ornament, securing with a rose bud.

Tussie Mussies

Victorian ladies knew the language of tussie mussies well. Each flower in the bouquet had a special meaning, and while courting, couples would send each other bouquets conveying their messages to each other. You can use the herbs and flowers in your own garden to make your own historical bouquet.

You will need:

A central flower (traditionally a large red rosebud)
Small flowers—lavender, pansy, marjoram, angelica, catmint violets, sweet peas, sage, tansy
Leaves—feathery ones such as fennel and southernwood, gray ones such as santolina. Rosemary, mint, balm, verbena, sweet-scented geraniums, etc.
Thin green string
Patterned paper doily and some ribbon

1. Holding the rosebud (or flower of your choice) firmly, place some of the smaller leaves around it in a tight circle and tie the stalks together with the green string to hold everything in place.

2. Encircle the little posy with small flowers and tie in place.

3. Finish off with a circle of the larger leaves and secure.

4. Make a hole in the center of the doily and poke the flower stems through. Settle this small bunch of flowers in place at the back of the doily and tie in place with long pieces of pretty ribbon. Curl the ends into streamers.

Reading a Tussie Mussie

Rose: I love you
Rosemary: Your presence revives me
Pansy: You are always in my mind
Angelica: You love lights up my life
Verbena: You enchant me
Thyme: All I want is to be with you
Sage: I will suffer anything for you
Marjoram: Your passion makes me blush
Agrimony: I am grateful
Forget-me-not: You are my true love
Lily-of-the-Valley: Happiness has returned
Ivy: I am true
Elder: I send compassion
Lemon Balm: I offer you sympathy
Sweet Basil: Good wishes

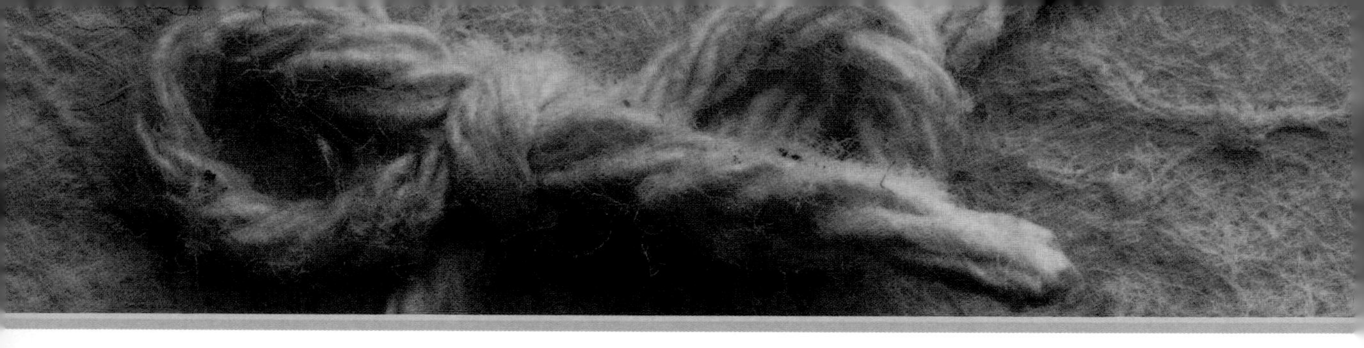

Herbal Paper

A textured paper with herbs embedded in the fibers makes a good mount for drawings, paintings, and photographs. Scented herbs in the fibers makes it an attractive drawer liner. Recycling computer print-outs and old newspapers tidies the place up and give trashs a new life.

1. Tear up the paper into small pieces and leave to soak overnight in warm water.

2. Make 2 wooden frames, writing paper size or larger to suit your need, and cover one of them tightly with strong nylon net.

3. The following day, liquidize the pulp in the blender, a little at a time. Use 2 3/4 cups of water to 3 tablespoons pulp plus a touch of starch to "size" the paper.

4. Pour it all into a deep, wide bucket or plastic bath.

5. Place the frame without net over the frame with net and, keeping them firmly together, dip them, vertically into the bucket.

6. Keeping the frames beneath the pulp, tilt them to the horizontal and lift upwards, slowly and steadily and bring them out of the pulp still at the horizontal.

7. Place on thick, spread newspaper to drain.

8. Take away the top frame and scatter your chosen herbs over the pulp. A thick scatter of scented potpourri will keep to make lovely drawer liners. Delicate flower petals, bits of dried fern, bits of torn onion skin, a single blossom, will make delightful paper for any purpose you please.

9. When the paper is dry, slide a palette knife underneath it and lift it carefully from the frame. The frame now has to be cleaned before it is used again.

Herbal Cards

Pressed flowers have been a popular herbal craft for centuries. Flower presses have been found in many Victorian-era homes. Press your own flowers, then share the beauty with these unique cards.

You will need:

2 sheets of parchment paper
2 heavy books
fresh herbal flowers
½ sheet of white card stock
crafting glue
thin ribbon

1. Rinse the flower(s), if needed.
2. Gently arrange the flower(s) onto one sheet of the parchment. Place the parchment on one of the books.
3. Be sure the flower is facing upwards and the stem is not bent, but slightly curved.
4. Top with the other parchment and book.
5. Leave pressed for 3–4 weeks, checking once a week.
6. The flower is finished when it is dry, but not brittle.
7. Fold the card stock in half, forming a card. Arrange the flower in the center of the card, attaching with a thin strip of craft glue.
8. Tie a bow with the ribbon and attach it to the bottom of the flower.
9. When the glue has fully dried, write your message on the inside of the card.

Note: One way to test for dryness is to feel the flower. If it feels cool to the touch, it is not dried.

Herbal Pillow

These herbal pillows can be decorated to match the bedroom or living room and can create a soothing relaxing environment. They can also be cooled and used as a compress.

You will need:

2 squares of decorative fabric, 10 x 10 inches (25 x 25cm)
quilting batting
1 cup chamomile flowers
1/2 cup lavender flowers
optional: trim

1. Double stitch three and a half sides of the cloth, adding the trim (if using).
2. Stuff with quilting batting and herbs scattered throughout.
3. Make sure the herbs are not poking towards the sides.
4. Pin and stitch the final section.

Other suggested mixtures:

Rose petals and lavender
Rosemary, mignonette, and rose petals
Verbena, marjoram, and lavender
Woodruff, mint, and chamomile
Scented geranium and rose petals
Peppermint, chamomile, and woodruff
Agrimony, woodruff and hops
Mint, balm, verbena and rose petals
Rose petals, lemon verbena, rosemary, and lavender

Herbal Flowers

Herbs produce the most beautiful floral blossoms. Next time flowers are called for, try making this fragrant herbal bouquet instead.

You will need:

fresh stems from any of the following plants:
verbena, thyme, feverfew, goldenrod, clary sage, rue, Black-eyed Susans, rosemary flowers, lavender, Echinacea, calendula, and yarrow
floral tissue paper (has a slight wax lining on one side of it)
wide satin ribbon

1. Arrange the stems with the largest centered on the tissue paper, moving outward to the smallest.
2. Wrap the paper around the bouquet and tie with the ribbon.

Note: Once given, herbal flowers can be treated as all other flowers. Just cut and place in a vase.

Calendula Picture Frame

Dried calendula keeps its color like very few herbs do. This makes it a perfect addition to a long-lasting keepsake, such as a picture. If you don't have any in your garden, look for calendula in your local health food store. The common name for calendula is marigold.

You will need:

unfinished wooden frame, 4 x 6 inches (10 x 15cm)
1 cup dried calendula flowers
hot glue gun
raffia

1. Begin gluing the largest flowers to the frame.
2. Fill up every inch of the wood with flowers, beginning with the largest flowers and finishing with the smallest.
3. Tie a small bow with the raffia and glue it to

KITCHEN

delicious butters, dips, and herbal vinegars to spice up any meal

Flavored Herbal Oils

Herbal oils make a welcome addition to many salad dressings, breads, and other recipes. While they are simple and easy to make, they leave a dramatic impression on the dish they have touched. The oil takes on the flavor of the herbs and can be used in salad dressings, marinades, breads—be creative with your recipes! Just take out a few to use for cooking as needed.

You will need:

dried herbs (garlic, rosemary or basil are great choices)
a glass bottle
virgin olive oil
cheesecloth

1. Place the herbs into the bottle. (You may need a wooden skewer to get them in.)
2. Pour olive oil into the bottle; be sure that the herbs are totally covered with oil.
3. Infuse for 2–3 weeks in a dark, cool space.
4. Strain the oil through the cheesecloth to remove the herb bits. Pour back into the bottle and label with the date and herbs used.

Suggested Uses:

Garlic oil: pizza dough, dinner rolls
Rosemary oil: dinner rolls, as a meat marinade
Basil oil: dinner rolls, oil and vinegar salad dressing

Herbal Butters

Nothing completes a meal like a flavored butter to top the meat or bread. Using culinary herbs, you can tie the entire meal together with a single main flavor or fragrance. These butters are simple to make and are best when left in the fridge overnight. They can also be stored in the freezer.

You will need:

1 pound (.5kg) organic or farm fresh butter
3 tablespoons dried herbs (rosemary, basil, and dill are my favorites)
3 tablespoons Parmesean or Romano cheese, grated (optional)

1. Soften butter at room temperature until pliable. Chop into 1-inch (2.5cm) cubes.
2. In a medium bowl, place the butter, herbs, and cheese (if using).
3. Beat on low speed until just blended.
4. Spoon into a small bowl or butter dish and serve, slightly softened.

The famous maitre d'hotel butter is made by beating lemon juice and some finely chopped parsley and chervil, (more chervil than parsley), into butter.

Easter Egg Dye

This year, go for a natural look and feel with herbal egg dyes. Herbs can create fresh, vibrant colors and are perfect for those who are sensitive to artificial dyes.

You will need:

vinegar
distilled water
herbs for colors (see below for a guide)
boiled eggs

1. For each color, mix 4 cups of water with 4 tablespoons of herb powder (or 3/4 cup of the whole herbs) and 3 tablespoons vinegar.
2. Bring to a boil and boil for 20–25 minutes.
3. Strain and cool.
4. Soak eggs for 10–15 minutes in the dye.
5. Dry in egg cups, then store in the fridge.

Color Guide

Purple: hibiscus flowers
Yellow: calendula petals
Orange: curry powder
Burnt: red chili powder
Pink: beet powder
Blue: red cabbage
Green: spinach powder or parsley powder

Herbal Vinegars

Give a new twist to your favorite salad dressing recipe with an infused vinegar. Infused vinegars have a long shelf life due to the natural preservation qualities of the vinegar, so you can leave them as a functional decoration in your kitchen.

You will need:

3–5 sprigs dried rosemary or basil
a dark, decorative bottle, preferably with a cork seal
cider vinegar (enough to fill your bottle)

1. Squeeze the sprigs of herbs into the bottle.
2. Pour vinegar over the herbs to within 1 inch from the top.
3. Cap tightly and let sit for 2–3 weeks away from direct sunlight.
4. At this point you can drain the herbs or leave them in for a fresh look and feel.

Other suggested combinations:

Basil, borage, and salad burnet
Basil, chives, lovage, and thyme
Balm and tarragon

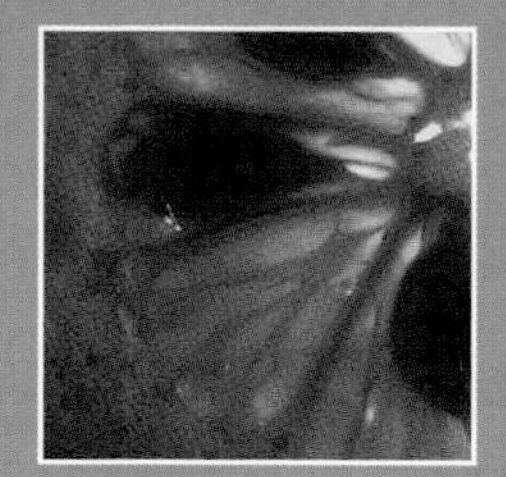

Herbal Ice Cubes

These ice cubes add a kick to summertime lemonade or iced tea. They are fun for kids to make and to blend with their favorite flavors. Try using mint for lemonade or parsley for iced tea.

You will need:
an ice cube tray
fresh herbs of choice: basil, chives, cilantro, fennel, lovage, mint, oregano, parsley, rosemary, sage, tarragon, thyme, etc.

1. Place a small flower or sprig into each opening in the ice cube tray.
2. Fill the tray 3⁄4 full with boiling water (this will blanch the herbs before freezing and will help them retain their flavor and color). (It's okay if the herbs "poke" out of the water.)
3. Freeze until ready to use.

Sugared Herbs

Show off your culinary skills with these gourmet additions to baked goods. Sugared herbs add a festive touch and lend an intriguing flavor to your baked confections.

You will need:

organic sugar
egg white (whipped)
edible flowers (If you do not grow your own, look for them at your local farmers market or gourmet grocery.)
clean paint brush or basting brush

1. Gently wash and dry flowers, while preheating oven to 175°F.
2. Place them face up on a cookie sheet lined with parchment.
3. Gently brush the egg white onto the leaves.
4. Dust with organic sugar.
5. Place in oven. Leave the door open and turn the oven off. Flowers should dry, but not turn brown.

Herbal Bread Dip

Herbal oils are perfect paired with a crusty artisan bread and a Mediterranean meal. Try different herbs to complement the flavors of the dish.

1. In a shallow bowl, crush the black pepper and sea salt together.
2. Add the herbs, and gently stir.
3. Pour the oil over and allow the mixture to stand 5–10 minutes to mellow.

Italian Herbal Dip

You will need:

¼ cup extra virgin olive oil
¼ teaspoon dried basil
¼ teaspoon dried oregano
dash sea salt
dash freshly ground black pepper

Mediterranean Herbal Dip

You will need:

¼ cup extra virgin olive oil
¼ teaspoon dried rosemary
¼ teaspoon dried thyme
dash sea salt
dash freshly ground black pepper

Drying Herbs

To dry herbs, cut them midmorning at the base of their stems. Loosely tie together with ribbon or raffia and store upside down, away from direct sunlight.

Kitchen Wreath

This is one of my favorite projects. It is as functional as it is decorative. All the herbs I need are just a snip away.

You will need:

straw wreath as a base (12-inch/30cm works well)
floral wire
raffia
floral tape
the following herbs, dried with the entire stems:

- *dill*
- *thyme*
- *oregano*
- *lavender*
- *sage*
- *basil*
- *bay*
- *rosemary*

1. With each herb, bunch together 2–3 groups of sprigs and tie together with the floral tape.
2. Grouping like herbs together, begin attaching bunches to the wreath base with the floral wire. Be sure all the stems are pointed the same way.
3. The last group of sprigs will have to be tucked into the flowers of the first applied.
4. Tie a bow across the bottom of the wreath with raffia.

Mulling Ciders

Nothing says Christmas to me like the scent of cider mulling over the stove. This childhood favorite serves double duty as a potpourri for the kitchen.

You will need:

1/2 gallon (2L) apple cider
4 cinnamon sticks
8 whole cloves
6 star anise (whole)

In a large pot, over the lowest heat, stir the spices with the cider for an hour or longer.

EUCALYPTUS

BODY CARE

bath tea, massage oil, neck wraps and more natural treatments

Relaxing Bath Tea

Herbal baths have been popular for centuries. The famed Roman baths often included herbs or herbal oils. Herbal bathing is a luxury that is still enjoyed around the world for relaxing and cleansing the body. Add salts to the bath to relax the muscles and soothe the skin.

You will need:

muslin tea bags
1/4 pound (113g) of each of the following dried herbs: chamomile, orange peel, lavender
sea salt or Epsom salts

In a large bowl, stir together the herbs and salts. Pour the blend into a dark-colored bottle or deep jar. Cap and label with the ingredients and date.

To use: Scoop about a fourth of a cup into the muslin bag and steep in the bath.

Invigorating Bath Tea

This bath tea is loaded with energizing herbs, making it a great pick-me-up.

You will need:

muslin tea bags
1/4 pound (113g) of each of the following dried herbs: lavender, basil, rosemary, sage

In a large bowl, stir together the herbs. Pour the blend into a dark-colored bottle or deep jar. Cap and label with the ingredients and date.

To use: Scoop about a fourth of a cup into the muslin bag and steep in the bath.

Lavender Bath Salts

For thousands of years, people have traveled long distances to reach natural salted baths. Now we can enjoy that luxury in our own homes! The addition of lavender brings stimulating properties that are wonderful after a long tiring day. For beautiful salts, look for the large chunks of sea salt.

You will need:

2 pounds (1kg) sea salts
⅓ cup lavender buds, dried
1 cup Epsom salts
25 drops essential oil (lavender)
glass bottle(s)

1. In a large bowl, blend together the salts and essential oil.
2. Gently blend in the lavender buds.
3. Pour mixture into bottle(s), cap, and store in a dry place.
4. Pour 1/2 cup into a warm bath.

Herbal Salt Glow

Salts are readily available in many forms. They come from seas around the world and can take on the character of their native land. They also make a great exfoliant or "scrubber"!

You will need:
a decorative jar
1 cup sea salt, fine
⅔ cup olive oil
¼ cup chamomile flowers
¼ cup marigold flowers (a.k.a. calendula flowers)

1. In a blender, chop chamomile and calendula flowers until a coarse powder.
2. In a separate bowl, stir salt with oil until thoroughly blended.
3. Stir in the coarse flower powder.
4. Spoon into the waiting jar and cap tightly.

Chamomile and calendula contain anti-inflammatory properties, which make them a great compliment to the sometimes rough sea salts. Look for them in your natural foods store, if you do not grow them in your garden.

Oatmeal Rose Bath

Soothing oatmeal has long been used by herbalists and traditionalists for soothing irritated skin. Red rose petals are a fragrant and luxurious addition to this soothing bath.

You will need:

1 cup rolled oats (not instant)
1 cup dried rose petals
½ cup dried milk powder
10 drops sweet orange essential oil
decorative bottle(s)

1. In a blender, chop oatmeal, milk, and half of the roses to a fine powder.
2. Move mixture to a large bowl.
3. Stir in the essential oil, blending well.
4. Stir in the remaining rose petals.
5. Pour into bottle(s), cap, and store in a dry place.
6. Pour 1/2 cup into a warm bath.

Lavender Basil Bath Oil

Bath oils not only add aromatherapy benefits to a warm bath, but the base oil, called a carrier oil, also helps to lock in the moisture from the bath. Be careful with bath oils, as they can be very slippery!

You will need:

½ cup apricot kernal oil
½ cup grape seed oil
25 drops lavender essential oil
15 drops basil essential oil
decorative bottle (to hold 1 cup)

1. Pour the apricot kernal oil and grape seed oil into the bottle.
2. Cap and shake to blend.
3. Add the essential oils to the oil blend, cap, and shake to blend.
4. Use 1–2 tablespoons per warm bath.

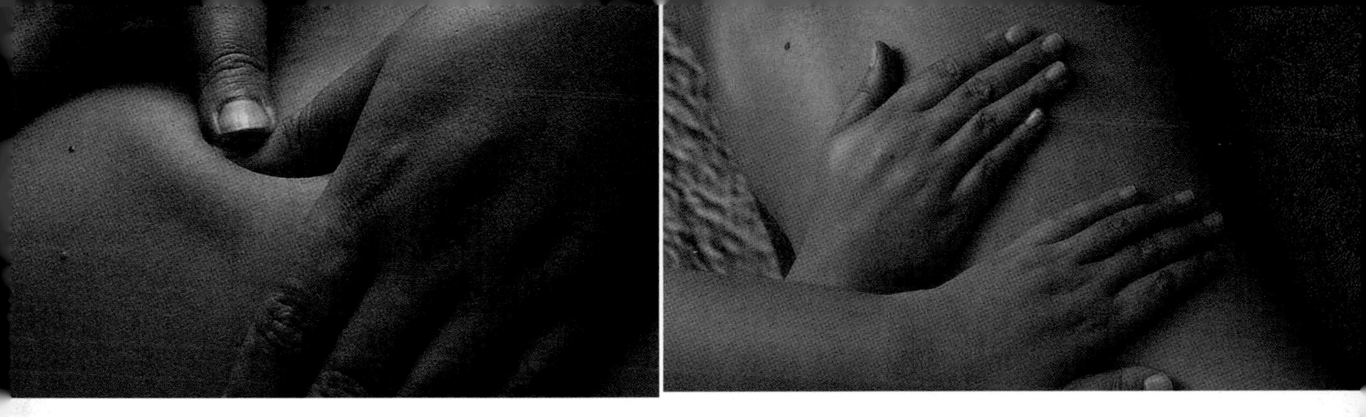

Sore Muscle Massage Oil

A good massage works wonders on tired muscles. Whether you've been in the garden all day or at the gym, this oil makes a welcome treat even more indulging.

You will need:

4-ounce (113g) dark glass bottle
2 ounces (57g) olive oil
2 ounces (57g) apricot kernal oil
⅛ cup chamomile flowers (dried)
15 drops lavender essential oil
10 drops peppermint essential oil
piece cheesecloth

1. Infuse the olive oil with the chamomile by leaving the flowers in the oil 2–4 weeks.
2. Strain the flowers with a muslin cloth or cheesecloth.
3. Pour both oils into the glass bottle.
4. Add the essential oils, cap, and shake well to blend.

Lavender Water

Lavender water in a pretty bottle with sprigs of lavender makes a delightful present.

You will need:

3 teaspoons lavender oil
1 cup surgical spirit
1 drop lavender essential oil

Mix ingredients and store in an airtight jar for 2 weeks, shaking the jar every now and then. Strain through fine muslin and bottle.

Lavender Soap Marbles

Small balls of sweet-scented soap for traveling and for guests are easily made.

You will need:
a bar of unscented good quality soft white soap
some lavender water
a touch of lavender essential oil

1. Grate the soap finely. Heat 2 1/2 tablespoons lavender water and pour over the soap. Leave for a while to let soap begin to dissolve. Stir well.

2. Add 2–3 drops lavender essential oil and put in the blender.

3. Blend until smooth. Pour into a basin and leave until you can see the soap is beginning to dry.

4. Take out a small quantity and roll it into a ball between the palms. Continue doing this until all the soap is used. You will know best the size of the marble or ball that will be most useful. Leave balls in a warm or sunny spot to dry.

5. When the balls are almost dry, pour some lavender water containing the merest trace of lavender essential oil on to the palms of the hands and roll the balls between them to give a final polish and scent.

Eye Pillow

These little pillows are perfect with a warm bath or relaxing massage. For a fresh feel, keep them in the fridge and apply as a cool compress.

You will need:

2 rectangles of cotton cloth, 11 x 4 inches (27 x 10cm)
1/4 cup each dried lavender and chamomile
10 drops sweet orange essential oil
1/2 cup rice

1. Double stitch three sides of the cloth, making sure they are well sealed.
2. In a medium bowl, toss herbs, rice, and oil until thoroughly blended.
3. Fill the pillow with this blend.
4. Pin and stitch the final side, taking care to seal the edges well.

The pillow can be refreshed by reheating in a microwave on medium heat for 20 to 25 seconds.

Neck Wrap

This little treat makes a great travel companion or gift for a frequent flyer. At home, toss in the microwave for 30 seconds for a warm compress or keep in the fridge for a cool soothing wrap.

You will need:

2 5 x 15-inch (13 x 38cm) cotton strips
2 cups rice
1/3 cup peppermint
1/2 cup chamomile
1/3 cup lemon balm

1. Double stitch three sides of the cloth, making sure they are well sealed.
2. In a medium bowl, toss herbs and rice until thoroughly blended.
3. Fill the wrap with this blend.
4. Pin and stitch the final side, taking care to seal the edges well.

Chamomile Moisture Bar

Homemade soaps are fun to make, and add a natural, herbal feel to the powder room or guest bath.

You will need:
10 ounces (283g) melt and pour soap
½ cup chamomile flowers
½ ounce (14g) apricot kernal oil
10 drops lavender essential oil (optional)
soap molds

1. Melt the soap according to the manufacturer's directions.
2. Quickly stir in the apricot kernal oil and the chamomile flowers.
3. When well blended, add the essential oil, if using.
4. Pour into molds to cool.

Soap molds can be purchased at your local craft supply store, or you can make your own. Cardboard juice concentrate cans, mini muffin tins, or even heavy-duty ice cube trays can be used as molds. Be sure they are strong enough to handle the high heat of the melted soap.

Gardening Bar

This colorful bar is loaded with exfoliants and skin soothers to cleanse and pamper your hands after an afternoon in the herb garden.

You will need:

10 ounces (283g) melt and pour soap
⅓ cup ground oatmeal
⅓ cup blue cornmeal (available at gourmet grocers)
⅓ cup lavender buds
10 drops lavender essential oil
12 drops grapefruit essential oil
soap molds

1. Melt soap according to manufacturer's instructions.
2. Stir in the oats and cornmeal until thoroughly blended.
3. Gently fold in the lavender flowers.
4. Stir in the essential oils.
5. Pour into soap molds.

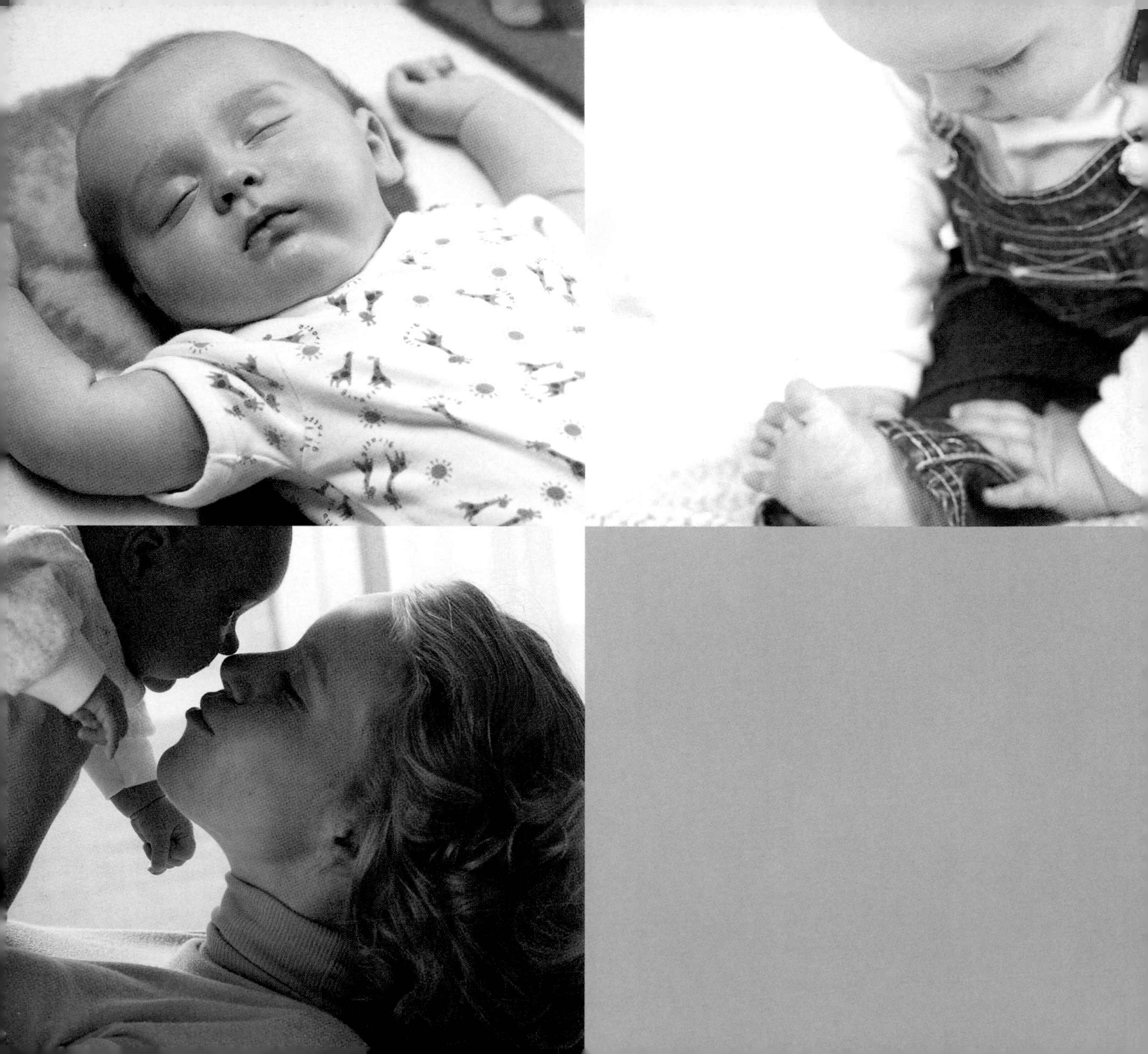

BABY

pamper your baby with natural, soothing herbs

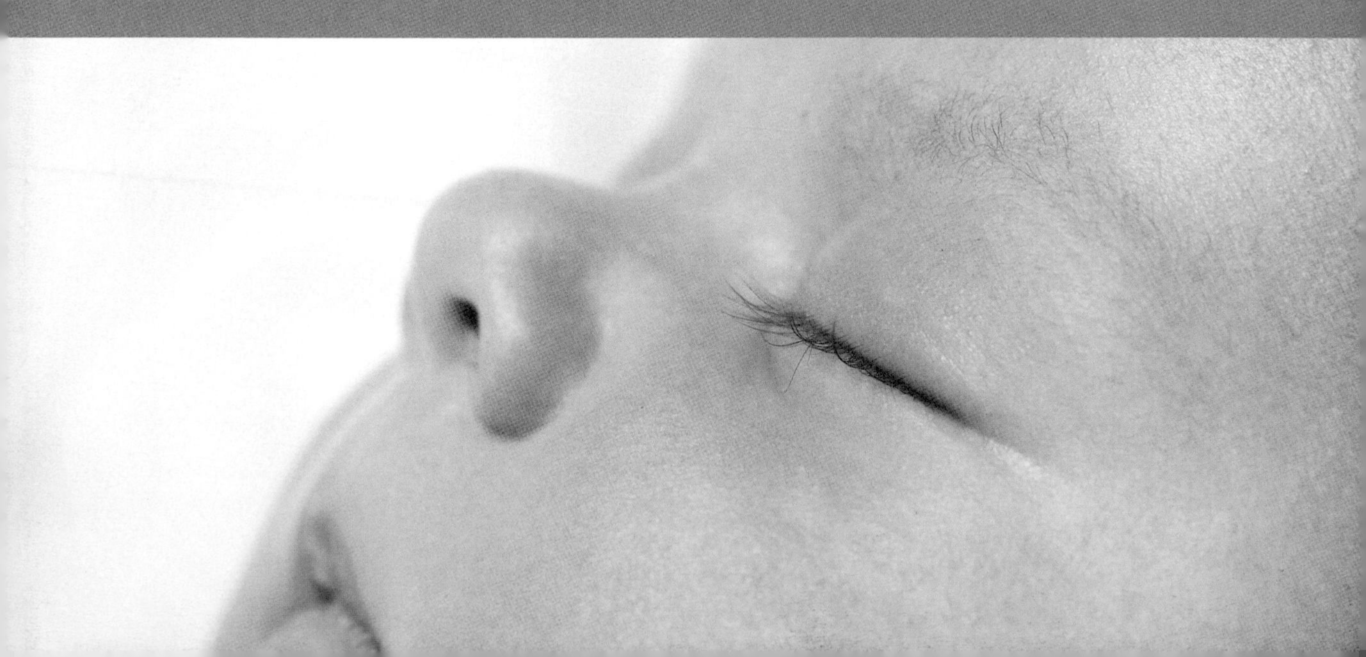

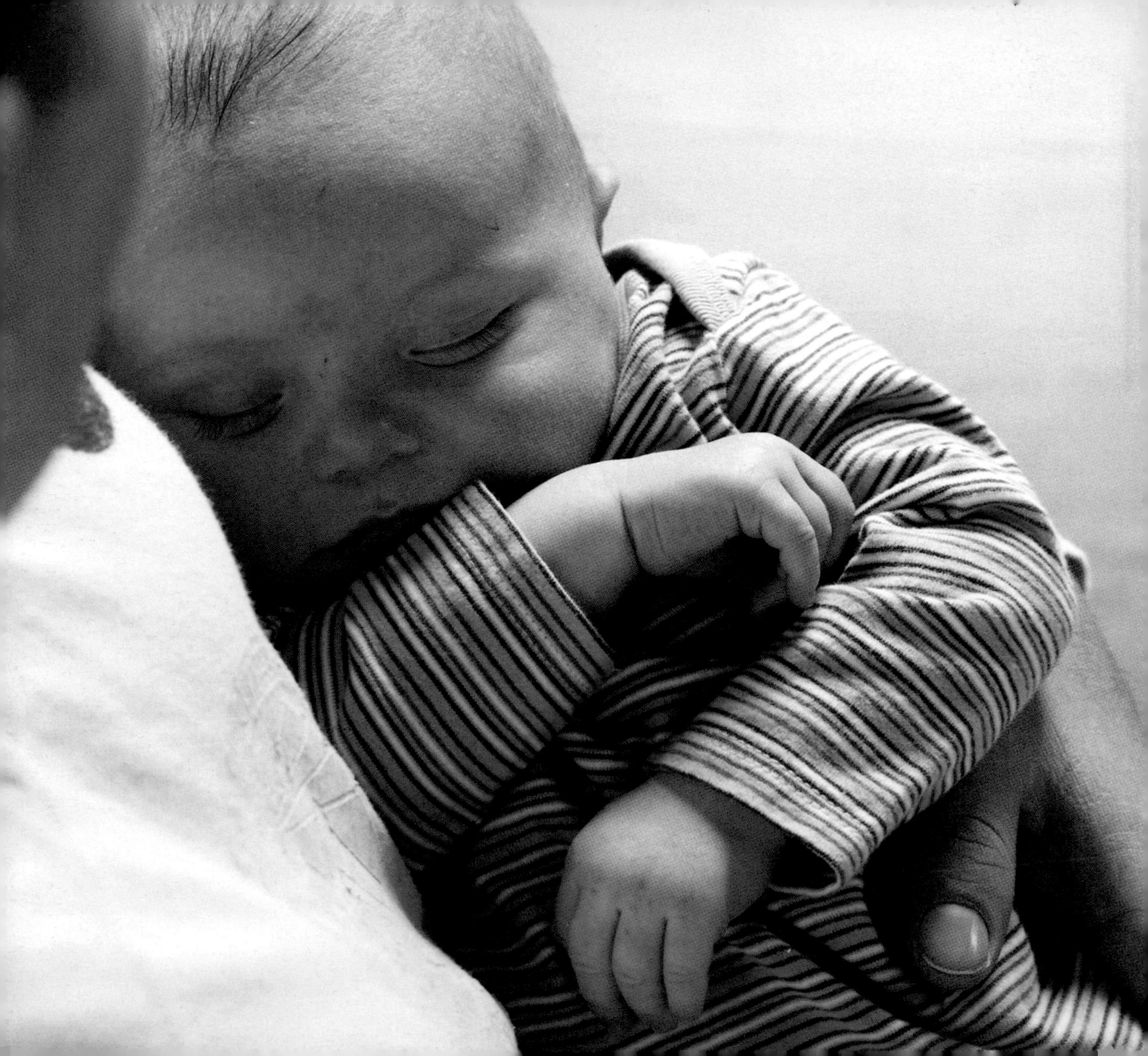

Nighty-Night Massage Oil

Baby massage can be fun for both mommy and baby. My babies love this special time with mommy and certain motions can actually calm and soothe babies.

You will need:

2-ounce decorative bottle
1 ounce apricot kernal oil
½ ounce olive oil
½ ounce coconut oil
12 drops lavender essential oil

Pour all the oils into the jar, including the essential oils. Cap and shake well to disperse the essential oils and blend all oils together.

Calming Baby Sachets

These sachets are perfect for adding to the baby's clothing drawer or closet. The herbs are calming herbs traditionally used to create a sleeping environment.

You will need:

6 4-inch squares of a light cotton cloth, such as unbleached muslin
1 cup chamomile
¼ cup hops
2 drops lavender essential oil

1. Pair up the cloth into three sets of 2 pieces each. Stitch together 3 sides of each sachet, leaving one side open to fill with the herbs.
2. In a large bowl, stir together the herbs and essential oil.
3. Divide into 3 parts and scoop into the bags.
4. Stitch the final side of the sachet together.

Basic massage instructions: Place baby on your lap, facing you. Gently effleurage from the tummy upward to the chest, then out towards the arms. Continue up the arms towards the fingers. Turn the baby over using one hand to support him or her. With the other hand, gently begin near the backside working upward towards the neck. Remember not to apply pressure; a gentle stroke is all that babies need.

Hops was first used in sleeping pillows in 1787 by King George III. During illnesses, hops pillows were used instead of the traditional opiates to help the king sleep.

Nursery Room Spray

Air fresheners are not always a great idea in a nursery, due to the baby's brand new sinuses. On the other hand, a new baby's room is just the room in need of a good freshening up. This gentle spritz is a perfect balance between caring for the babies new bodily systems and taking care of your own sense of smell.

You will need:

2–4-ounce glass spray bottle
distilled water
¾ teaspoon lavender essential oil
1 teaspoon sweet orange essential oil
½ teaspoon lemon essential oil

1. Fill the bottle with the distilled water, leaving an inch from the top.
2. Add the oils and shake well to blend. Cap and label with date and ingredients.
3. Spritz room as needed, taking care to shake the bottle well before using.

Herbal Baby Powder

Baby powder slides in and out of fame as the key ingredient to a diaper change. Talc, a main ingredient, is suspected to cause allergies in the new baby's little nose. This talc-free powder keeps babies safe while providing the parents with the nostalgia they love.

You will need:

½ cup arrowroot powder
2 tablespoons loose calendula petals
2 tablespoons loose chamomile petals
10 drops lavender essential oil
½ cup white cosmetic clay (also known as kaolin clay)

1. In a blender, grind the flower petals into a fine powder.
2. Add the clay and arrowroot powder and blend well.
3. Mix in the essential oil and scoop into a sifting bottle or a wide-mouth jar with a powder duster.

Soothing Balm

Soothing balms are very useful with the large number of diapers a newborn goes through. Most pediatric experts agree that babies need nothing added to their skin for the first 4 months of age, but sometimes the bum needs a little protection. This soothing balm contains very few ingredients reducing the chances of a reaction on the new baby's skin.

You will need:

2 ounces grape seed oil
½ ounce beeswax
45 drops chamomile extract
45 drops slippery elm bark extract
15 drops lavender essential oil
small tin container of other heatproof jar

1. Mix the beeswax and oils together in a microwave-safe dish.
2. Melt on medium heat, stirring every 30 seconds.
3. When totally melted, work quickly to add the extracts and essential oil, stirring well to ensure that it is blended.
4. Pour into the jar and cap tightly.

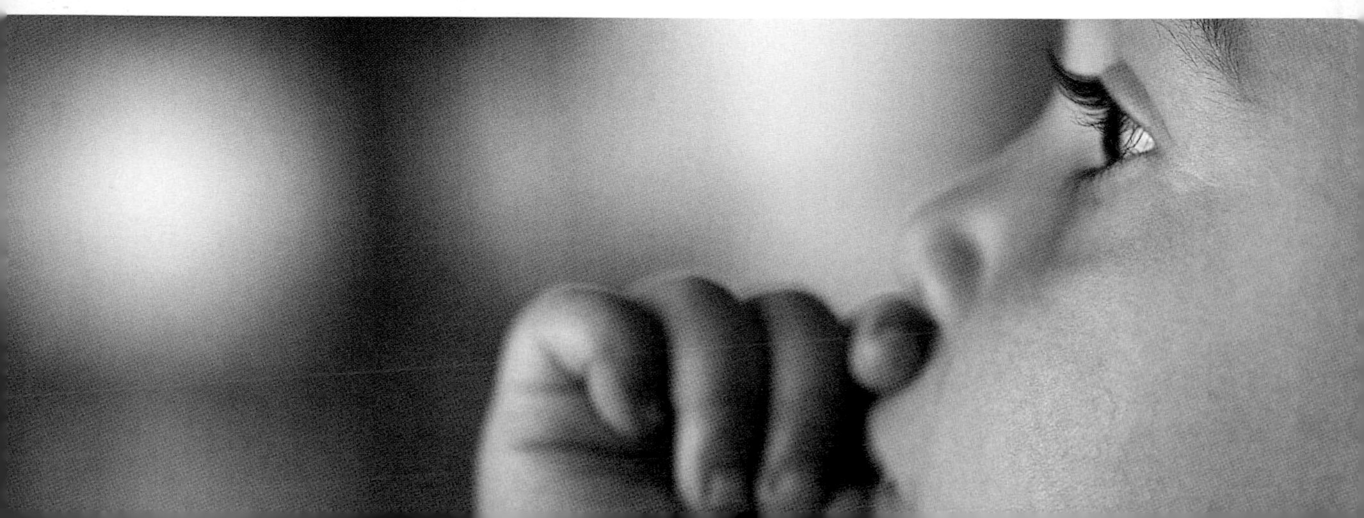

Belly Oil

Mommy's growing belly needs lots of love and attention. During this special time, a soothing belly oil is just the trick as a gentle massage oil and moisturizer to keep the skin supple.

You will need:

¼ olive oil
¼ apricot kernal oil
½ coconut oil
4-ounce glass bottle
optional: 15 drops essential oil (Remember to use a baby and mommy-safe oil. In general, the lighter oils are best—spearmint instead of peppermint, for example. Lavender and orange oils are also good choices. And if mommy has nausea, the natural coconut scent may be best.)

1. Scoop the coconut oil into a large bowl and stir to soften. (This step is not needed during warm months.)
2. Add the other oils (and essential oil, if using).
3. Stir thoroughly to blend.
4. Scoop or pour into the glass bottle. Add a label with the ingredients and date.

Coconut oil—often called coconut butter—melts at 76°F, which means that in the cooler months, this oil will be more firm then in the summer.

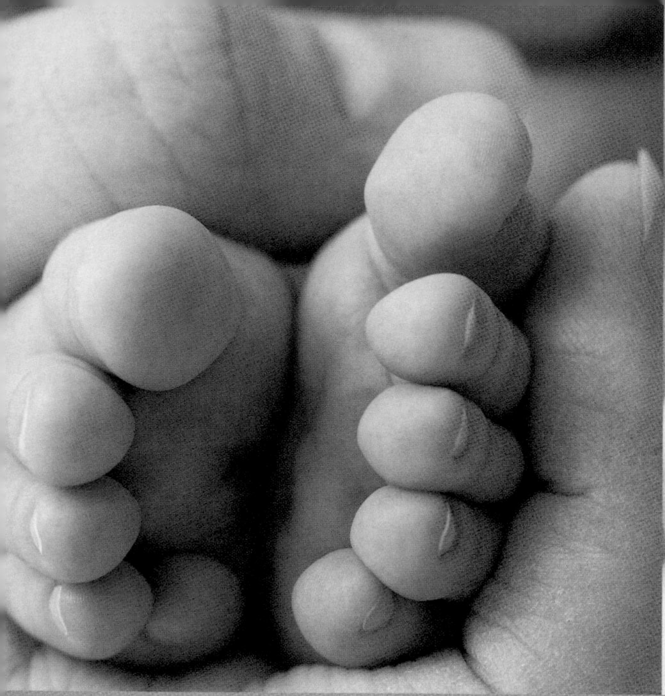

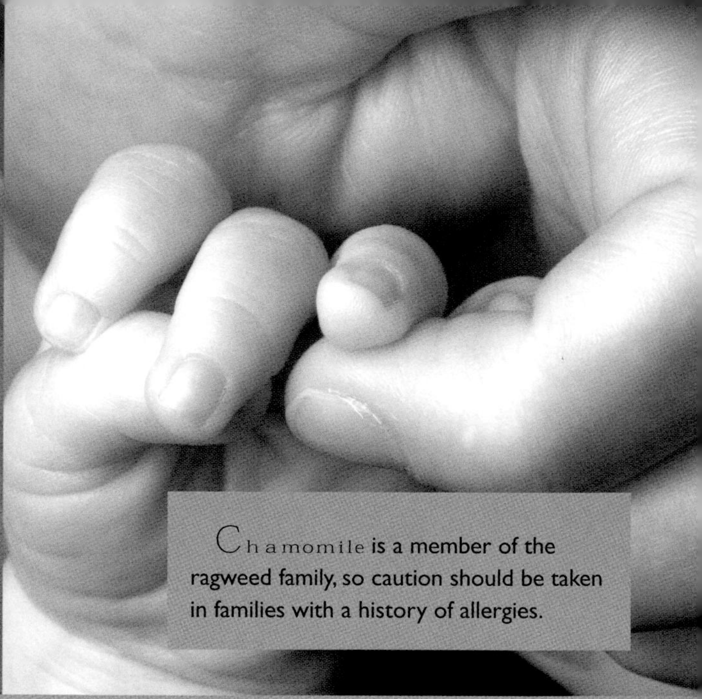

Chamomile is a member of the ragweed family, so caution should be taken in families with a history of allergies.

Chamomile Baby Bath Tea

Chamomile is famous for its soothing and calming properties. Its apple-like scent makes it a popular favorite and the anti-inflammatory properties are just right for older babies.

You will need:
muslin tea bags (available at health food stores)
dried chamomile flowers
decorative jar

1. Sift flowers, removing stems and any loose non-floral pieces. Place into a decorative jar.
2. Scoop two teaspoons of the dried flowers into the muslin bag and "steep" in a warm bath.
3. Remove bag before placing baby in bath.
4. Rinse and reuse muslin bags.

Gentle Washing Scents

I never use synthetic fabric softeners on my new baby's clothing, but I love adding a light scent to the wash. These scents are my way of freshening the wash without adding harsh irritants. Many essential oils also contain antibacterial properties, so these are a great way of boosting the cleansing power in the wash.

You will need:

½-ounce glass bottle, with a dropper-style top
25 drops of each essential oil: tea tree, eucalyptus
50 drops of each essential oil: lavender, sweet orange

Drop each of the oils into the half-ounce jar. Shake well to mix.

To use: Drop 10 drops into the rinse cycle (where you normally would fabric softener).

Note: Essential oils are very potent. Do not store in plastic or drop directly onto a baby's clothes or the washing machine.

Marigolds, also known as calendula, retain their colors, even when dried. After this annual finishes its flowers for the year, the flowers can be dried out and made into a long-lasting keepsake, such as the calendula frame on page 49.

Birth Announcements

These cute little announcements not only announce the new birth, but they also offer the family a long-lasting keepsake of the new life.

You will need:

1 page of white card stock
handmade paper (available at fine art supply stores)
marigold seeds
Elmer's glue
3 x 4 sheet of tissue paper

1. If using a printer, print the details of the birth onto the card stock before cutting.
2. Cut the card stock into halves, and fold each one into a 4.25 x 5.5-inch card.
3. Glue the tissue paper to the front of the card.
4. Arrange the seeds on the outside of the tissue paper.
5. With a solid coating, glue the edges of the handmade paper to the edges of the tissue paper, sealing the seeds loosely in the middle.
6. Include these instructions on sprouting: "Place the entire packet, tissue included, 1/4 inch deep into a flower pot full of well nourished soil. Water into place. As your little sprout grows, you can be reminded of our little sprout growing in his first year."

Drying Herbs

The aim is to dry the herbs keeping as much of their color and flavor as possible so the sooner the drying can begin the better. Loss of moisture must be gradual and steady—a quick frizzle will result in a pile of brown dust. A dried leaf should still be green, but brittle, and easily stripped, whole, from the stem. If it crumbles when touched, it has been overdone. Two to three days to a week or more, depending on the size and thickness of the material being dried is usual.

⌘ Try not to wash herbs before use.

⌘ A dry, warm, airy spot, away from the light is ideal for drying herbs.

⌘ A shed with an open, shuttered door—a room with open shuttered windows—a space under the house—but not a garage because the herbs will be affected by gas fumes. And not the kitchen—steam from the cooking will do them no good at all.

⌘ Bunches of herbs hung to dry should be small, a dozen stems at most, and one type of herb only to each bunch. Secure the bunch with string or an elastic band. String is better. Tie the stems safely but not too tightly (air must be able to flow through the bunches or mold will take hold) and make a loop. Hang the loop with the herbs head downwards from a hook where air can flow all round them—not against a wall.

⌘ If you have to wash herbs before drying them, let them hang, head down until as much water as possible has drained away, then separate them into small bunches. Tie each one separately and put the head downwards into a brown paper bag, large enough to give air space all around the heads and tie the bag in place. Hang in a warm, dry place until the contents of the bag rustle. You will probably have to finish the drying in a slow oven.

⌘ If you are going in for drying in a big way, search around for an old-fashioned clothes rack—the kind that used to hang in the kitchen and could be let down and drawn up. It will hold dozens of bunches at a time.

⌘ If you were to store it under the house, for instance, it would be wise to tie an open-bottomed paper bag around each bunch as protection against dust.